DEVIN
AND HIS MAGICAL
EARS

WENDY YVETTE DEJESUS

DEDICATION

This book is dedicated to my amazing family and our mom, Thelma Stilson

Hawkins.

The rain had stopped, and the sun was shining.

This rainbow came with a silver lining!

The story was told, that it came with a boy and no pot of gold.

The most beautiful baby that they'd ever seen, mommy and daddy thought, "oh, what a dream!" His eyes sparkled as blue as the sky, and a smile so bright, it lit up the night.

This little boy was sent from heaven, and he went by the name of Baby Devin!

He was perfect, they thought right away, but he didn't hear all that they'd say!

This didn't matter; they just didn't care, the love in their hearts was what they wanted to share.

They used their hands to communicate, and for a while, that was great, but the days passed, and Devin got a bit older, so they bought him a gift to help him hear bolder.

They said they were magic and the key to all sound, but he felt different on the playground.

They put his magic ears in every day, but Baby Devin would just toss them away!

The journey began one day on the block, when Devin and his cousin Eddy were out for a walk.

Eddy was long-legged, thin, and freckled. She was always sad because she often got heckled.

She was as cute and sweet as a kid could be, but she had spaghetti for hair, not like you and me.

"Eddy spaghetti with the meatball eyes," the kids would taunt.

"I hate my hair! Spaghetti? Seriously? How unfair!"

Eddy was tired of the kids making fun, it hurt her heart, and she wanted to run.

Devin nodded and agreed, for spaghetti hair, there was no need.

He felt her pain and pointed to his ears, and looked at Eddy as she fought back tears.

"I hear there's a man who lives on the hill, who will grant us wishes, deliver happiness and goodwill.

"No more concern or care how we look, just that fairy tale ending, like in all books.

The only thing is that he is not near, we must travel through the forest of fear."

They decided that day to leave at dawn, to head up the mountain, their troubles soon to be gone.

They woke up early and gathered their things, excited to see what this day would bring.

They headed out towards the trail, but first they saw Papa Delay out tending the bail.

The Delay's house smelled of apple pie and coffee cakes. Mr. Delay was out front with his rake.

Two little kids sat on the lawn, Cora and Vinney, but Robyn was gone. "Where are you headed?" he asked with delight.

"To change all our flaws and make everything right."

"You are both perfect; no flaws do I see, but be sure to say hi to Robyn, from mother and me."

They began their trek up the mountain, and who did they see?

Their other cousin they called WP3.

"Why are you here?" he asked right away.

"We must reach the top by the end of the day."

"The forest is scary, I wouldn't move on, there are too many dangers from this moment on."

"You're always so nervous and scared of all things, you should come with us and see what it brings."

He agreed, and off they went. They looked up the mountain and began their ascent.

As they reached the peak, so out of breath they couldn't speak.

They took a moment to look around.

They stared in amazement at the place they had found.

There he was, the man they were after, this vision of peace some called Master.

There was Robyn sitting on the wise man's shoulder.

You could tell by her smile she had done what he told her.

Once a Robin who was scared to fly now stood tall and soared through the sky.

"You have all come because you don't like what you see. You must look within, surely not at me. Gratitude and acceptance are what need to be done, you will then love yourself and most everyone. You are all special in great ways, embrace your differences and be on your way."

He whispered kindly and with composure, but this didn't help, they still had no closure.

Back down the mountain, they lose sight of the course.

This journey seemed pointless and filled with remorse.

Devin was hungry and needed to eat, but no one packed food, so there were no treats.

"We're all going to starve; we aren't going to make it.

I'm so scared, I'm not going to fake it."

"What will we do? We also can't see!" Fright in his eyes, poor WP3.

They continued along, and just ahead, an armadillo lay comfy in bed.

"What is your name? They asked with a smile. "Ami the Armadillo, I've been here for a while."

"You live in Deedles dungeon all alone?"

"No, I was with Tewkie the tortoise, and this was our home."

"We came up here when we fell ill; we were sad, scared, and totally unprepared."

"We went to the peak, and who did we seek? The man on the mountain, who was hairless like me, but he had no sadness that I could see, just peace, love, and tranquility."

I asked, "Dear sir, why did this happen to me?

I can't handle the pressure, this can't you see?"

"I don't have the answers; I wish I knew why. Sometimes there's no reason I'm not gonna lie." He said, "Search for the good; this you must try."

"It took me a while, but then I did see, all the love that came, from that thing that happened to me."

"Tortoise and I, we grew so close, she was my best friend and the one I loved most, she was my why, and I'll never forget, the bond that we made and the day that she left."

"Embrace your strengths and accept your lack, and this is all you will need to find your way back."

They said their goodbyes and started to leave. Something felt different, like what they set out to achieve.

Eddy leaped up, "I have an idea to end our despair, we will be fine by eating my hair. In the past, my hair was a big problem, but today is the day it will definitely solve them!"

"I am so proud of what I've done; this hair has finally helped someone!

"We must listen for the river. It's our only way home," WP3 said with an excited tone. "It's fine to be scared and have fear at the start. It's the courage we need, and it's here in our hearts."

Devin leaned over, turned up the sound, and pressed his ears to the ground. He signed, "I got it! Follow close by, my ears ARE magic! That was no lie."

He could hear the river flow loud and clear. "This way, guys, it's fairly near!"

A smile on his face and joy in his heart, he thought to himself, "well, this is a start, I have used my ears to do my part. I may be different and that's ok, but different can often save the day."

Now full of confidence and headed in the right direction.

All the things that they thought held them back, were no longer an imperfection.

All the faults they once possessed are now what make them feel their best.

The sun begins to rise, and a new day starts. They came out different and with love in their hearts.

They saw the opening of the path and some familiar faces yelled "Finally! At last!"

Their families were all there in delight. Glad they were safe and made it through the night, Papa on his tractor, happy as can be and on his lap, Eddy's sister, Little Miss Cora Lee.

Vinny came screaming and gave a big hug. WP3 felt all the love.

"Brother, please don't ever go, Dad, and I missed you more than you know."

"I had to do it; so many things became clear I learned to have courage in the presence of fear."

"Mom, Dad, you were not wrong; my ears WERE magic all along."

They went up the mountain to change all their flaws, but then accepted themselves for just who they are.

All their differences that they thought were wrong, were the very things that made them all strong.

A family's love, as strong as can be, nothing will break them, now this you see!

Devin and his Magical Ears, is a realistic fiction book based on my family, who I am beyond proud to call mine.

All the characters and their nicknames are all real. Although some of the story is completely made up, it is loosely based on real life events and troubles we've had to conquer through out the last few years.

Its a story of courage, perseverance and learning to find your strength when life throws you curve-balls.

Printed in the USA
CPSIA information can be obtained
at www.ICGtesting.com
LVHW081214140124
768656LV00008B/568